You're Born An Original, Don't Die A Copy!

by

John Mason

10th Printing
Over 145,000 in Print

You're Born An Original, Don't Die A Copy!
ISBN 0-88419-355-1
Copyright © 1993 by John Mason
Published by Insight International
P.O. Box 54996
Tulsa, Oklahoma 74155

Contents

DEDICATION

I am proud to dedicate this book to my wonderful wife, Linda, and our four great kids Michelle, Greg, Mike and Dave.

To Linda, for her prayers, agreement and encouragement.
To Michelle, for her ideas.
To Greg, for his patience.
To Mike, for his love of God's creation.
To Dave, for his happy spirit.

Without their love, support and originality, this book would have never happened.

ACKNOWLEDGMENTS

It is impossible to write a book like this one without the help of some "divine connections." Special thanks to three outstanding originals:

Mike Loomis, who has encouraged me as much as any other person to be an original, to look to the future, and to finish this book.

Tim Redmond, whose words always leave a positive investment in me. And who I'm honored to quote several times in this book.

Tom Winters, whose life has impacted me to be a man of character and integrity.

INTRODUCTION

One of the great blessings in my life is the privilege of speaking many times each year throughout the country. Because of this, I spend a fair amount of time in airports. As I walk through these terminals, I am always moved by the hundreds of people in a hurry to nowhere. My heart not only goes out to this mass of people, but also to some specific individuals.

I wish I could stop them and ask, "Do you realize God has a unique plan for your life? Did you know that He "packaged" you perfectly for the job? Are you aware that His best is a life of peace, abundance, satisfaction, and love?

That's why I wrote this book. First, to attack the mediocrity of doing anything other than what God wants you to do. Secondly, to stir up the gifts He has placed within you!

I know that you've entrusted to me one of your most precious resources, your time. I promise to do my best to be a good steward of the minutes we spend together. That is why I wrote this book in fifty-two nuggets of truth like my first book, *An Enemy Called Average*. You won't have to wait ten pages to get one point, you'll find ten points on one page.

My prayer as you read this book is that God will reveal His plan for you, stir up what He's put inside you and cause you to take action towards the great plan He has for your life.

LOOKING
INWARD

NUGGET # 1

How Many Outstanding Generalities Do You Know?

How many outstanding people do you know with unique and distinctive characteristics? Don't be a living custard. It's true what Eric Hoffer said: "When people are free to do as they please, they usually imitate each other." Man is the only creation that refuses to be what he is.

Don't just look for miracles. You are a miracle. You are "fearfully and wonderfully made" (Ps. 139:14). Do not be awestruck by other people and try to copy them. Nobody can be you as efficiently and as effectively as you can. When you fully use the gifts you have, people call you gifted. One of the hardest things about climbing the ladder of success is getting through the crowd of copies at the bottom.

You are a specialist. You are not created to be all things to all people. More than 90 percent of all flowers have either an unpleasant odor or none at all. Yet it is the ones with sweet fragrance that we most remember. Stand out! "Following the path of least resistance is what makes men and rivers crooked," says Larry Bielat. Too many people make cemeteries of their lives by burying their talents and gifts.

The copy adapts himself to the world, but the original tries to adapt the world to him. "Don't copy the behaviors of this world, but be a new and different person with a fresh newness in all you do and think. Then you will learn from your own experience how His ways will really satisfy you" (Rom. 12:2, LB).

It doesn't take a majority to make a change—it takes only a few determined originals and a sound cause. You're the only one in all of creation who has your set of abilities. You're special...you're rare. And in all rarity there is great worth. You are not insignificant; you are valuable and precious. God loves you just the way you are, but He loves you too much to leave you the way you are.

"Could Hamlet have been written by a committee, or the Mona Lisa painted by a club? Could the New Testament have been composed as a conference report? Creative ideas do not spring from groups. They spring from individuals. The divine spark leaps from the finger of God to the finger of Adam," said A. Whitney Griswold.

While an original is always hard to find, he is easy to recognize. God leads every soul in an individual way. There are no precedents: You are the first You that ever was. There is not enough darkness in the whole world to put out the light that God has put in you.

YOU ARE AN ORIGINAL.

NUGGET #2

Passion Is The Spark For Your Fuse.

God has put inside every person the potential to be passion-ate. One person with passion is greater than the passive force of ninety-nine who have only an interest. Too many people have "only an interest" in their destiny. The book of Ecclesiastes says, "Whatsoever thy hand findeth to do, do it with all thy might" (9:10).

Everyone loves something. We are shaped and motivated by what we love. It is our passion. Ignore what you are passionate about, and you ignore one of the greatest potentials that God has put inside you. Nothing significant was ever achieved without passion. Jesus was a passionate man. He died for us because He loved us passionately.

Most winners are just ex-losers who got passionate. The worst bankruptcy in the world is the person who has lost his enthusiasm, his passion. When you add passion to a belief, it becomes a conviction. And there is a big difference between a belief and a conviction. Belief agrees with the facts. Conviction brings persistent action to your belief.

Driven by passionate conviction, you can do anything you want with your life—except give up on the thing you care about. My friend Mike Murdock said, "What generates passion and zeal in you is a clue to revealing your destiny. What you love is a clue to something you contain."

Fulfilling God's plan for your life is a passion or it is nothing. We are told to, "Serve the Lord thy God with all thy heart and with all thy soul" (Deut. 10:12). "Without passion man is a mere latent force and a possibility, like the flint which awaits the shock of the iron before it can give forth its spark," (Henri Frederic Ameil). Pessimism never won any battles. "There are many things that will catch my eye, but there are only a very few that catch my heart...it is those I consider to pursue," said Tim Redmond.

LET THE PASSION THAT IS WITHIN YOU RISE TO MEET YOUR DESTINY.

NUGGET #3

Questions

"Who said it?" is an important question to ask of everything we believe.

Do you make promises or commitments?

Do you make friends before you need them?

Does God seem far away? If so, guess who moved?

Who's creating your world?

Do you have a strong will or a strong won't?

The last time you failed, did you stop trying because you failed—or did you fail because you stopped trying?

What is it like to be my friend?

What is it like to work with me?

Are you making a living or a life?

If the future generations were dependent on you for spiritual knowledge, how much would they receive?

Do you risk enough to exercise your faith in God?

Do you say "our Father" on Sunday and then act like an orphan the rest of the week?

Are you willing to preach what you practice?

Does failure discourage or bring determination?

Do you exist, or do you live?

Is God your hope or your excuse?

What dominates your day?

How many people have you made homesick to know God?

Is your mission on earth finished?

How many happy selfish people do you know?

How many people do you know who became successful at something they hate?

What force is more potent than love?

"Is there anything too hard for the Lord?" (Gen. 18:14).

If you were arrested for being kind, would there be enough evidence to convict you?

What is more miserable than being out of God's will?

NUGGET #4

Fear Wants You To Run From Something That Isn't After You.

The great evangelist Billy Sunday once said, "Fear knocked at my door. Faith answered...and there was no one there." That's the proper response to fear. Why does fear like to take the place of faith? The two have a lot in common—both believe that what you cannot see will happen. Faith ends where worry begins, and worry ends where faith begins. Our worst imaginations almost never happen, and most worries die in vain anticipation. "It ain't no use putting up your umbrella till it rains," said Alice Caldwell Rice.

What you fear about tomorrow is not here yet. "Don't be afraid of the day you have never seen," (English Proverb). Fear holds you back from flexing your risk muscle. It's been said that worry is a darkroom where negatives are developed. Like a rocking chair, it keeps you going, but you don't get anywhere. If you can't help worrying, remember that worrying can't help you either. A friend of mine once said, "Don't tell me that worry doesn't do any good. I know better. The things I worry about don't happen."

Most of our fears can be traced back to a fear of man. But the Bible says that "The Lord is the strength of my life; of whom then shall I be afraid?" (Ps. 27:1). "In God I trust; I will not be afraid. What can mortal man do to me?" (Ps. 56:4, NIV). People would worry less about what others think of them if they only realized how seldom they do.

Most people believe their doubts and doubt their beliefs. So do like the old saying and "feed your faith and watch your doubts starve to death." Many people are so filled with fear that they go through life running from something that isn't after them. Fear of the future is a waste of the present. Fear not tomorrow. God is already there. Never be afraid to trust an unknown future to a known God.

Follow Howard Chandler's advice when he said: "Every morning I spend fifteen minutes filling my mind full of God; and there's no room left over for worry thoughts." A famous old poem in The Prairie Pastor said it best: "Said the robin to the sparrow, I should really like to know why these anxious human beings rush about and worry so. Said the sparrow to the robin, I think that it must be they have no Heavenly Father such as cares for you and me."

DON'T BE AFRAID TO BE YOU.

NUGGET #5

From This Page You Can Go Anywhere You Want To.

Do you know what this page is noted for? This page is the springboard to your future. You can start here and go anywhere you want to.

God has placed within each of us the potential and opportunity for success. Yet it takes just as much effort to lead a bad life as it does a good life. Still, millions lead aimless lives in prisons of their own making—simply because they haven't decided what to do with their lives. It always costs more not to do God's will than to do it. In fact, "a lot of people confuse bad decision-making with destiny" (Kin Hubbard).

The Bible says, "Where there is no vision the people perish" (Proverbs 29:18). That's not God's plan for you. Dissatisfaction and discouragement is not the absence of things but the absence of vision.

When you are an original and walk in God's plan, you shine like a star in the firmament. Copies are like the darkness in which they float. You can predict a person's bright future by his awareness of his destiny. Life's heaviest burden is to have nothing to carry. The significance of any person is determined by the cause for which he lives and the price he is willing to pay. What you set your heart on will determine how you spend your life.

Do not take lightly the dreams and hopes God has given for your life. Cherish them, for they are like children birthed within you. "It is better to die for something than it is to live for nothing," says Dr. Bob Jones, Sr. A man without principle never draws much interest.

No wind blows in favor of a ship without a destination. A person without a conviction is like a ship without a rudder. People generally have too many opinions and not enough convictions. God plants no yearning in you that He does not intend to satisfy. We distrust our hearts too much and our heads not enough. As long as God's direction is your friend, don't worry about your enemies. It is not the man with a motive but the man with a purpose who prevails. "Every man's destiny is his life preserver." (The Sunday School).

LAUNCH OUT!!

NUGGET #6

You're Like A Tea Bag — Not Worth Much Till You've Been Through Some Hot Water.

Have you ever failed or made a mistake? Good, then this nugget is for you. The fact that you've failed is proof that you're not finished. Failures and mistakes can be a bridge, not a barricade, to success.

Psalms 37:23-24 says, "The steps of a good man are ordered by the Lord: and he delighteth in his way. Though he fall, he shall not be utterly cast down: for the Lord upholdeth him with his hand." Failure may look like a fact, but it's just an opinion. It's not how far you fall but how high you bounce that makes all the difference.

Theodore Roosevelt said, "Far better it is to dare mighty things, to win glorious triumphs, even though checked by failure than to rank with those poor spirits who neither enjoy much nor suffer much because they live in the gray twilight that knows not victory or defeat." One of the riskiest things you can do in life is to take too many precautions and never have any failures or mistakes.

No one ever achieved worthwhile success who did not, at one time or another, teeter on the edge of disaster. If you have tried to do something and failed, you are vastly better off than if you had tried to do nothing and succeeded. The person who never makes a mistake must get awfully tired doing nothing. If you're not making mistakes, you're not risking enough.

23

Success consists of getting up just one time more than you fell down. "You don't drown by falling in the water; you drown by staying there," said author Edwin Louis Cole. So get up and go on. Proverbs 28:13 (LB) says, "A man who refuses to admit his mistakes can never be successful, but if he confesses and forsakes them, he gets another chance."

The death of your dream will not be accomplished by a major failure. Its death will come from indifference and apathy. The best way to go on after a failure is to learn the lesson and forget the details.

Failure can become a weight or it can give you wings. The only way to make a comeback is to go on. If the truth were known, 99 percent of success is built on former failure.

Remember the old poem that says, "Success is failure turned inside out, the silver tint of the clouds of doubt, and you never can tell how close you are, it may be near when it seems so far. So stick to the fight when you're hardest hit, it's when things seem worse that you must not quit," (Unknown).

YOU HAVE A FORMER FAILURE WITH SUCCESS WRITTEN ALL OVER IT.

NUGGET #7

You Can Never See The Sunrise By Looking To The West.

How you position yourself to receive makes all the difference. For example, as you read this book, if you position yourself to receive by saying to the Lord, "I will take action on what You show me," you will benefit more than if you read it just to be motivated or inspired. Action springs not from thought, but from a readiness for responsibility. Position yourself to be ready for responsibility.

I've known many people who were excellent reservoirs of learning yet never had an idea. "Eyes that look are common. Eyes that see are rare," says J. Oswald Sanders. The problem is we're flooded with information and starving for revelation.

To resist or receive is a choice we make every day. Nothing dies quicker than a new idea in a closed mind. It is impossible for a man to learn what he thinks he already knows. I believe that Jesus responded strongly to the Pharisees because they refused to position themselves to receive.

Availability is the greatest ability you have. The devil trembles when he hears God's weakest servant say, "Yes, Lord I'll do it!" When you're facing God, your back is turned to the devil. Never give up control of your life to anything but faith.

Our walk with God begins with the word "Follow" and ends with the word "Go!" The opportunities God sends won't wake up those who are asleep. "Kneeling is the proper posture for putting seeds into the ground," says Brooks Atkinson. The Christian on his knees sees more than the world on its tiptoes.

Opportunities can drop in your lap if you have your lap where opportunities drop. When you don't position yourself to receive, it's like praying for a bushel but only carrying a cup. Don't pray for rain if you're going to complain about the mud.

We typically see things, not as they are, but as we are. By how we position ourselves, we will see the evidence of God everywhere or nowhere. Too often our minds are locked on one track. We are looking for red, so we overlook blue; we are thinking tomorrow, and God is saying now; we are looking everywhere, and the answer is under our nose.

When a person is positioned correctly, he is ready to receive all that God has for him.

POSITION YOURSELF FOR ACTION.

NUGGET #8

The Person With Imagination Is Never Alone And Never Finished.

You were created for creativity. Your eyes look for opportunity, your ears listen for direction, your mind requires a challenge and your heart longs for God's way.

Make a daily demand on your creativity. Everything great started as somebody's daydream. All people of action are first dreamers. The wonder of imagination is this: It has the power to light its own fire. Ability is a flame, creativity is a fire. Originality sees things with fresh vision. Unlike an airplane, your imagination can take off day or night in any kind of circumstances. Let it fly!

First Corinthians 2:16 says, "We have the mind of Christ." Don't you know we've been given a part of His creativity too.

A genius is someone who shoots at a target no one else sees and hits it. "We are told never to cross a bridge till we come to it, but this world is owned by men who have 'crossed bridges' in their imagination far ahead of the crowd," (Speakers Library). We should observe the future and act before it occurs.

Many times we act, or fail to act, not because of will but because of imagination. Your dreams are an indicator of your potential greatness, and you'll know it's a God-given idea because it will always comes to you with the force of a revelation.

Grandmother saw Billy running around the house slapping himself and asked him why. "Well," said Billy, "I just got so tired of walking that I thought I'd ride my horse for a while." One day Michelangelo saw a block of marble which the owner said was of no value. "It is valuable to me," said Michelangelo. "There is an angel imprisoned in it, and I must set it free."

Other people may be smarter, better educated or more experienced than you, but no single person has a corner on dreams, desire or ambition. The creation of a thousand forests of opportunity can spring from a tiny acorn of an idea. "No man that does not see visions will ever realize any high hope or undertake any high enterprise," said Woodrow Wilson.

The Bible says, "Where there is no vision the people perish" (Prov. 29:18). Not being a person of imagination causes your life to be less than it was intended to be. A dream is one of the most exciting things there is. Your heart has eyes which the brain knows nothing of. You are more than an empty bottle to be filled. You are a candle to be lit. Light the fire of your imagination.

INSIDE YOU THERE'S A CREATIVE IDEA WAITING TO BE RELEASED.

NUGGET #9

Decision Determines Destiny.

The Bible says that a double-minded man is unstable in all his ways (James 1:8). I know people who are triple and quadruple-minded...I don't know what they are. It's not the difference between people that's the difficulty, it's the indifference. All around us, fools seem to be growing without watering. Too many people spend their lives failing and never even notice.

God wants us to be the most decisive people on the face of the earth. Why did He give us His Word and the Holy Spirit? So that we can live decisive lives! How can the Lord guide a man if he has not made up his mind which way he wants to go? All of us are at fault for all of the good we didn't do. "The average man does not know what to do with this life, yet wants another one which will last forever," said Anatold France.

The most unhappy people are those who can never make a decision. An indecisive person can never be said to belong to himself. Don't worry about not making a decision; someone else will make it for you. You can't grow while letting others make decisions for you. Indecisive people are like a blind man looking in a dark room for a black cat that isn't there.

The devil is the only one who can use a neutral person. Jesus said in Matthew 12:30, "He who is not with me is against me, and he who does not gather with me scatters." Making no decision is a decision. It does not require a decision to go to hell. "Mistrust the man who finds everything good, the man who finds everything evil

29

and, still more, the man who is indifferent to everything," says Larry Bielat.

Meet all the problems and opportunities of your life with decision. A great deal of talent is lost for want of a little decision. "Decision is a sharp knife that cuts clean and straight; indecision is a dull one that hacks and tears and leaves ragged edges behind," says Gordon Graham.

Faith demands a decision before it can work. Every accomplishment great or small starts with a decision. Not everything that is met can be changed, but nothing can be changed until it is met.

You'll have the wrong foundation and won't know what to do if you're indecisive. The Bible says, "If ye will not believe, surely ye shall not be established" (Is. 7:9). "If the trumpet giveth an uncertain sound, who shall prepare himself to the battle?" (1 Cor. 14:8).

Remain indecisive, and you will never grow. To move on from where you are, decide where you would rather be. Decision does determines destiny.

WHAT IS ONE DECISION
YOU MUST MAKE?

NUGGET #10

Start With What You Have, Not What You Don't Have.

God has already given you what you need to begin to create your future. Yet most of us have found ourselves saying, "If only I had this...if only this were different...if only I had more money, then I could do what God wants me to do," all the while ignoring the seeds that God has planted within us. People always overstate the importance of things they don't have. God will never ask you for something you can't give Him. He wants you to start with what He has given you.

Don't let what you cannot do keep you from doing what you can do. Prolonged idleness paralyzes initiative. To the vacillating mind, everything is impossible because it seems so. Do not wait for extraordinary circumstances to do good; use ordinary situations. We don't need more strength, ability or greater opportunity. What we need is to use what we have.

"The lure of the distant and the difficult is deceptive. The great opportunity is where you are," said John Burroughs. What you can do now is the only influence you have over your future. True greatness consists of being great in little things. Don't grumble because you don't have what you want; be thankful you don't get what you deserve. " 'We must do something' is the unanimous refrain. 'You begin' is the deadening reply," said Walter Dwight.

No person can ever be happy until he has learned to use what he has and not worry over what he does not have. Happiness will never come to those who fail to appreciate what they already have. Most people make the mistake of looking too far ahead for things close by.

You can never get much of anything done unless you go ahead and do it before you are ready. No one ever made a success of anything by first waiting until all the conditions were "just right." The Bible says in Ecclesiastes 11:4 (LB), "If you wait for perfect conditions, you'll never get anything done."

Don't waste time in doubts and fears about what you don't have; spend yourself in the task before you, knowing that the right performance of this hour's duties will be the best preparation for the years that follow it. "Grow where you are planted. Begin to weave, and God will give the thread," (German Proverb).

JUST DO IT...WITH WHAT YOU HAVE.

NUGGET #11

Destiny Delayed Is The Devil's Delight.

The most important moment in your life is right now. Don't let hesitation and procrastination keep you from your destiny. Procrastination is the symptom, fear is the problem. When you delay your duties, you delight the devil.

Be jealous of your time; it is your greatest treasure. Ideas have a short shelf life–that's why we must act before the expiration date. Procrastination is the ability to keep up with yesterday. "Even if you're on the right track–you'll get run over if you just sit there," says Arthur Godfrey. Putting off a simple thing makes it hard, and putting off a hard thing makes it impossible.

Obedience is God's method of provision for your life. "If ye are willing and obedient, ye shall eat the good of the land" (Is. 1:19). Obedience brings blessings. Delayed obedience is disobedience. Obedience means at once. Discouragement always follows a decision to delay action.

Today is the day to start. It's always too soon to stop. Many times we're not to understand, just obey. The quickest way to get out of the hole is to obey God. There is a reason why God revealed the idea to you today. "We ought to obey God rather than men," (Acts 5:29). Choosing to obey men is what keeps us from being instant to obey God. Be instant to obey, taking action without delay. What most folks need is an alarm clock that will ring when it's time for them to rise to the occasion.

Why don't we jump at opportunities as quickly as we jump at conclusions? Procrastination is the grave in which opportunity is buried. Anybody who brags about what he's going to do tomorrow probably did the same thing yesterday. Few things are more dangerous to a person's character than having nothing to do and plenty of time in which to do it. Killing time is not murder, it's suicide. Two things rob people of their peace of mind: work unfinished and work not yet begun.

Opportunity is often lost in the deliberation. "Good resolutions are like babies crying in church; they should be carried out immediately," says Charles M. Sheldon. Tackle any difficulty at first sight, for the longer you gaze at it the bigger it becomes. The lazier a person is, the more he is going to do tomorrow. The tragedy of life is not that it ends so soon, but that we wait so long to begin it.

KILL PROCRASTINATION, NOT TIME.

NUGGET #12

There Are No Unimportant People.

You are not insignificant. Never view your life as if Jesus did nothing for you. Make the most of yourself, for that is all that God made of you. The first and worst of all frauds is to betray yourself. If you deliberately plan to be less than you are capable of being, you will bring unhappiness to the rest of your life.

Too many people never begin to do what God wants them to do because they are waiting to be able to sing like Sandi Patti, preach like Billy Graham or write like Chuck Swindoll before they start. God knew what He was doing when He put you together. Use what talents you possess. The woods would be very silent if the only birds that sang were those that sang the very best.

You were created for achievement. You have been given the seeds for greatness. What is greatness? What is achievement? It is doing what God wants you to do and being where He wants you to be.

Christians are new creations, not rebuilt sinners. Don't ever forget that God calls you a friend (see John 15:15). What an incredible statement that is! He also says you are "wonderfully made" (Ps. 139:14).

You're beginning to see that God made you special for a purpose. He has a job for you that no one else can do as well as you. Out of the billions of applicants, only one is qualified, only one has the right combination of what it takes. God has given each person the measure of faith to do what He has called them to do. Every person is gifted.

A person is never what he ought to be until he is doing what he ought to be doing. God holds us not only responsible for what we have, but for what we could have; not only for what we are, but for what we might be. Man is responsible to God for becoming what God has made possible for him to become.

Your life makes a difference. Although we're all different, no mixture is insignificant. On judgment day, God won't ask me why I wasn't Joshua or Billy Graham or Pat Robertson but why I wasn't John Mason. Jerry Van Dyke said it best when he said, "The best rose bush is not the one with the fewest thorns, but that which bears the finest roses."

YOU ARE THE BEST PERSON TO DO
WHAT GOD HAS CALLED YOU TO DO.

NUGGET #13

Don't Build A Case Against Yourself.

What does God think about your future? We find the answer in the book of Jeremiah (29:11, NIV): "I know the plans I have for you, declares the Lord, plans to prosper you and not to harm you, plans to give you a hope and a future." All of what we are, good and bad, is what we have thought and believed. What you have become is due to the price you paid to get what you used to want.

All of the important battles we face will be waged within ourselves. Nothing great has ever been achieved except by those who dared believe that God was superior to any circumstance. First John 4:4 says, "Greater is he who is in you than he who is in the world."

Don't put water in your own boat; the storm will put enough in on its own. Don't dream up thousands of reasons why you can't do what you want to; find one reason why you can. It is easier to do all the things you should do than spend the rest of your life wishing you had. The first key victory you must win is over yourself. "You can't consistently perform in a manner that is inconsistent with the way you see yourself," says Zig Ziglar.

Building a case against yourself is like a microscope–it magnifies trifling things but cannot receive great ones. To keep from building a case against yourself: multiply your prayer time, divide the truth from a lie, subtract negative influences and add God's Word. We lie loudest when we lie to ourselves. Both faith and fear may sail into your harbor, but allow only faith to drop anchor.

DISMISS ALL THE CASES
YOU'VE MADE
AGAINST YOURSELF.

NUGGET #14

You Can't Walk Backward Into The Future.

It is more valuable to look where you're going than to see where you've been. Don't see your future only from the perspective of yesterday. It's too easy to quantify and qualify everything and choke off or limit the dream within you.

"The past should be a springboard, not a hammock," said Edmund Burke. You can never plan the future by the past. No one can walk backward into the future. Those to whom yesterday still looks big aren't doing much today.

Your future contains more happiness than any past you can remember. The born-again Christian has no past. Second Corinthians 5:17 (NIV) says, "Therefore, if anyone is in Christ, he is a new creation; the old has gone, the new has come!" God doesn't look at your past to decide your future.

"Misery is a yesterday person trying to get along with a tomorrow God," says Mike Murdock. Don't let your past mistakes become memorials. They should be cremated, not embalmed. It is important to look forward—your calling and destiny are there. The apostle Paul said, "Forgetting what is behind and straining toward

39

what is ahead, I press on toward the goal to win the prize for which God has called me heavenward in Christ Jesus" (Phil. 3:13-14, NIV).

Those who predominantly talk about the past are going backward. Those who talk about the present are just maintaining. But those who talk about the future are growing.

Some people stay so far in the past that the future is gone before they get there. The future frightens only those who prefer living in the past. No one has ever backed into prosperity. You can't have a better tomorrow if you are thinking about yesterday today. Yesterday has passed forever and is beyond our control. What lies behind us is insignificant compared to what lies ahead.

THE PAST IS PAST.

NUGGET #15

Go Out On A Limb — That's Where The Fruit Is.

Be bold and courageous. When you look back on your life, you'll regret the things you didn't do more than the things you did. When facing a difficult task, act as though it is impossible to fail. If you're going to climb Mount Everest, bring along the American flag. Go from looking at what you can see to believing what you can have. Don't undertake a plan unless it is distinctly important and nearly impossible. Don't bunt–aim out of the ballpark.

The mediocre man thinks he isn't. "Not doing more than the average is what keeps the average down," says William M. Winans. "Undertake something that is difficult; it will do you good. Unless you try to do something beyond what you have already mastered, you will never grow," said Ronald E. Osborn. It is difficult to say what is truly impossible, for what we take for granted today seemed impossible yesterday. "Impossible," Napoleon is quoted as saying, "is a word found only in the dictionary of fools." What words are found in your dictionary?

He who is afraid of doing too much always does too little. To achieve all that is possible, we must attempt the impossible. Learn to be comfortable with great dreams.

The best jobs haven't been found. The best work hasn't been done. Christians are not to stay in the shadow but to stretch in the light of the Cross. He who expects nothing shall never be disappointed. "Is anything too hard for the Lord?" (Gen 18:14).

The readiness to take risks is our grasp of faith. God puts no restriction on faith; faith puts no restriction on God. "But without faith it is impossible to please Him" (Heb. 11:6). Your vision must be bigger than you. Let us say, "Lead me to the rock that is higher than I" (Ps. 61:2).

"Don't avoid extremes to stay 'in balance', stay in balance by living in the extreme that God wills at that time in your life," says Tim Redmond. Unless a man takes on more than he can possibly do, he will never do all that he can. "Brethren, be great believers. Little faith will bring your souls to heaven, but great faith will bring heaven to your souls," said Charles Spurgeon.

The most disappointed people in the world are those who get just what is coming to them and no more. There are a lot of ways to become a failure, but never taking a chance is the most successful. Some things have to be believed to be seen. Attempt something so fantastic that unless God is in it, it is destined for failure.

YOUR VISION IS YOUR POTENTIAL WORTH.

NUGGET #16

Be Like Babies...
They Like Changes.

The late astronaut James Irwin said, "You might think going to the moon was the most scientific project ever but they literally 'threw us' in the direction of the moon. We had to adjust our course every ten minutes and landed only inside fifty feet of the five hundred mile radius of our target." Life, like this trip to the moon, is full of changes. There is nothing so permanent as change.

"When you can't change the direction of the wind–adjust your sails," (Max DePree). We cannot become what we need to be by remaining what we are. He who stops changing ceases growing. People hate change, yet it is the only thing that brings growth.

Everyone wants to change the world, but no one thinks of changing himself. "Poverty and shame shall be to him that refuseth instruction: but he that regardeth reproof shall be honored" (Prov. 13:18). Unacceptance of the present creates a future. "Happy is the man whom God correcteth" (Job 5:17). "Better to be pruned to grow than cut up to burn," said John Trapp. A bad habit never goes away by itself. "It's always an undo-it-yourself project." (Abigail Van Buren)

Proverbs 13:19 (LB) says, "It is pleasant to see plans develop. That is why fools refuse to give them up even when they are wrong." Wise people sometimes change their minds–fools never do. Be open to God's change in your plans. It is a sign of strength to make changes when necessary.

The longer a man is in error, the surer he is he's right. Defending your faults and errors only proves that you have no intention of quitting them. An obstinate man does not hold opinions—they hold him.

Where we cannot invent we can at least improve. A "sensational new idea" is sometimes just an old idea with its sleeves rolled up. If you itch for ideas, keep on scratching. Everybody is in favor of progress. It's the change they don't like. Constant change is here to stay. Most people are willing to change, not because they see the light, but because they feel the heat.

Great ideas still need change, adaptation and modification in order to prosper and succeed. Henry Ford forgot to put a reverse gear in his first automobile. Few knew of his oversight. Few don't know of his success. Success and growth are unlikely if you always do things the way you've always done them.

CHANGE IS GOOD.

NUGGET #17

If You Continue To Do What's Right, What's Wrong And Who's Wrong Will Eventually Leave Your Life. (David Blunt)

A businessman had personalized letterhead that read: "Right is right even if everyone is against it, and wrong is wrong even if everyone is for it." James 1:12 (LB) says, "Happy is the man who doesn't give in and do wrong when he is tempted, for afterward he will get as his reward the crown of life that God has promised those who love Him."

Spend less time worrying about who's right and take charge of deciding what's right in your life. Don't let someone else choose it for you. Your failures may be planned by hell, but your victory is planned by heaven. "And remember when someone wants to do wrong it is never God who is tempting him, for God never wants to do wrong and never tempts anyone else to do it" (James 1:13, LB).

You cannot do the right thing too soon, for you never know when it will be too late. You can always find the time to do what you really want to do.

Successful people understand that no one makes it to the top in a single bound. What sets them apart is their willingness to keep putting one right step in front of the other, no matter how rough the terrain. We are what we repeatedly do.

Consider the words of John Wesley:

Do all the good you can,
In all the ways you can,
In all the places you can,
At all times you can,
To all the people you can,
As long as ever you can.

You draw nothing out of the bank of life except what you deposit in it. The height of a man's potential is in proportion to his surrender to what is right. People who live right never get left. Any act of disobedience lengthens the distance between you and your dream. Likewise, the realization of your dreams is accomplished by sustained prayer and right action.

DO WHAT'S RIGHT, THEN DO WHAT'S RIGHT, THEN DO WHAT'S RIGHT.

NUGGET #18

Failure Is Waiting On The Path Of Least Persistence.

Never give up on what you know you really should do. The person with big dreams is more powerful than the person with all the facts. Remember, overnight success takes about ten years. The "man of the hour" spent many days and nights getting there. Consider the man who said, "My overnight success was the longest night of my life."

Earl Nightingale said, "A young man once asked a great and famous older man, 'How can I make a name for myself in the world and become successful?' The great and famous man replied: 'You have only to decide upon what it is you want and then stay with it, never deviating from your course no matter how long it takes, or how rough the road, until you have accomplished it.'" Winners simply do what losers don't want to do. Success is largely a matter of holding on after others have let go.

In the confrontation between the stream and the rock, the stream always wins—not through strength but through perseverance. Christopher Morley said, "Big shots are only little shots that keep shooting." Persistence is simply enjoying the distance between the fulfillment of God's promises.

Judas was an example of someone who started the good fight of faith but lacked persistence. Many of the world's great failures did not realize how close they were to success when they gave up. Stopping at third base adds no more score than striking out. We rate success by what people finish, not by what they start. People do not fail, they just quit too easily.

God won't give up on you! Don't you give up on God! "For I am persuaded that neither death, nor life, nor angels, nor principalities, nor powers, nor things present, nor things to come, nor height, nor depth, nor any other creature, shall be able to separate us from the love of God, which is in Christ Jesus our Lord" (Rom. 8:38-39).

Your persistence is proof you have not yet been defeated. Mike Murdock says, "You have no right to anything you have not pursued. For the proof of desire is in the pursuit." So, "Commit to the Lord whatever you do, and your plans will succeed" (Proverbs 16:3, NIV). Life holds no greater wealth than that of steadfast commitment. It cannot be robbed from you. Only you can lose it by your will.

The destiny of the diligent is to stand in the company of leaders. "Seest thou a man diligent in his business? He shall stand before kings" (Prov. 22:29). When faithfulness is most difficult, it is most necessary, because trying times are no time to quit trying. The secret of success is to start from scratch and keep on scratching.

LET GO OF WHATEVER MAKES YOU STOP.

NUGGET #19

Focus Changes Everything.

First Corinthians 9:25 (LB) says, "To win the contest you must deny yourselves many things that would keep you from doing your best." Doing too many things always keeps you from doing your best. The best way to bring focus into your life is never to place a question mark where God has put a period.

One man with focus constitutes a majority. The person who begins too much accomplishes too little. If you wait to do a great deal of good at once, you will never do anything. He that is everywhere is really nowhere.

When you don't have focus life becomes painful and confusing. "Better is a handful with quietness, than both the hands full with travail and vexation of spirit" (Eccl. 4:6). When you don't have a good reason for doing a thing, you have one good reason for letting it alone. It's amazing the amount of work you can get done if you don't do anything else.

"Every human mind is a great slumbering power until awakened by a keen specific desire and by definite resolution to do," says Edgar F. Roberts. Focus is one of the most necessary ingredients of character, and one of the best instruments of success. Without focus, creativity wastes its efforts in a maze of inconsistencies.

Few things are impossible to diligence and focus. Whatever you focus your attention upon you give strength and momentum to. Focus is the secret of strength.

Jesus said in Luke 14:33, "Whosoever he be of you that forsaketh not all that he hath, he cannot be my disciple." Being a disciple of Christ requires focus. When you walk in focus, you'll become passionate about your dream; you'll find it expressed everywhere—you can almost smell it.

The focused straight and narrow way has the lowest accident rate. It is important that people know what you stand for; it is equally important that they know what you won't stand for. We cannot do everything we want to do, but we can do everything God wants us to do.

FOCUS IS FANTASTIC.

LOOKING
OUTWARD

NUGGET #20

Leave Everyone A Little Better Than You Found Them.

Proverbs 11:24-25 (LB) says, "It is possible to give away and become richer! It is also possible to hold on too tightly and lose everything." Yes, the liberal man shall be rich! By watering others, he waters himself. You were created to help others.

Those that are best at helping others are always able to see the bright side of other people's troubles. Practicing the Golden Rule is not a sacrifice, it's an investment. Don't give until it hurts, give until it feels good.

"What we do for ourselves alone dies with us; what we do for others is timeless. What I gave, I have; what I spent, I had; what I kept, I lost," (Old epitaph). No man is more deceived than the selfish man. "No man was ever honored for what he received. Honor has been the reward for what he gave," said Calvin Coolidge. Invest in the success of others. Because when you help someone up a mountain, you'll find yourself close to the summit too.

If you want others to improve, let them hear the nice things you say about them. People will treat you the way you view them. Find the good in everyone. Most people can smile for two months on five words of praise and a pat on the back. Draw out and stir up their gifts and callings

What good thing you make come to pass for others, God will make come to pass for you. "Knowing that whatsoever good thing any man doeth, the same shall he receive of the Lord" (Eph. 6:8).

You grow spiritually to the extent that you give out. By giving out, you create more room to grow on the inside.

"Give instruction to a wise man, and he will be yet wiser; teach a just man, and he will increase in learning" (Prov. 9:9). You may be the only Bible some people will ever read. Remember the words of D. L. Moody: "Where one reads the Bible, a hundred read you and me."

What means most in life is what you have done for others. It is the duty of all Christians to make it difficult for others to do wrong, easy to do right. "Those who bring sunshine to the lives of others cannot keep it from themselves," said James Matthew Barrie.

If you treat a person as he is, he will remain as he is. If you treat him as if he were what he could be, he will become what he could be. There is no exercise better for the heart than reaching down and lifting someone else up.

FIND SOMEONE TO HELP.

NUGGET #21

Don't Spend Your Life Standing At The Complaint Counter.

The person who is always finding fault seldom finds anything else. Live your life as an exclamation, not an explanation. Any complainer will tell you success is nothing but luck. Children are born optimists, and the world slowly tries to educate them out of their "delusion." The fact is, the more you complain the less you'll obtain. A life of complaining is the ultimate rut. The only difference between a rut and a grave is the timing. A complaining spirit is first a caller, then a guest and finally a master.

Some people always find the bad in a situation. Do you know people like that? How many successful complainers do you know? "Little men with little minds and little imagination go through life in little ruts, smugly resisting all changes which would jar their little worlds," (Anonymous). Small things affect small minds. Some people are confident they could move mountains if only someone else would just clear the rocks out of their way. Some of the most disappointed people in the world are those who get what is coming to them.

Misery wants your company. Complainers attract other complainers, while repelling positive people. When God gets ready to bless you He doesn't send complainers into your life. He sends those full of faith, power and love.

When you feel like complaining, bring God into the situation. You have to shut out His light to be in the dark. "Thou wilt keep him in perfect peace whose mind is stayed on thee" (Is. 26:3). Are you waiting on God , or is He waiting on you? Is God your hope or your excuse? Don't let heaven become only a complaint counter.

"Of all sad words of tongue or pen, the saddest are these: 'It might have been!" (John Greenleaf Whittier). Don't complain. The wheel that squeaks the loudest often gets replaced. If you complain about other people, you have no time to love them.

WHEN YOU COMPLAIN YOU EXPLAIN YOUR PAIN FOR NO GAIN.

NUGGET #22

If You're Green With Envy, You're Ripe For Problems.

One of the most valuable decisions we can make is not to compare our own lives with what is happening in other people's lives. What happens in someone else's life has nothing to do with what God is doing in yours. God loves you just as much as He loves others. "God is no respecter of persons," (Acts 10:34). Every time we put our eyes on other people, we take our eyes off God.

Some people seem to know how to live everybody's lives but their own. Envy is the consuming desire to have everybody else a little less successful than you are. Don't measure your success by what others haven't done. "Love envieth not" (1 Cor. 13:4). Jealousy is the tribute mediocrity pays to achievers. Criticizing another's garden doesn't keep the weeds out of your own.

Envy is a tremendous waste of mental energy. Refrain from it—it is the source of most unhappiness. If you're comparing yourself with others, your view is distorted. "Don't be content to be the chip off the old block, be the old block itself," (Winston Churchill). "Don't be a fraction, be a whole," (Greg Mason).

Don't surrender leadership of your destiny to outside forces. George Craig Stewart says, "Weak men are the slaves of what happens. Strong men are masters of what happens." The shoe doesn't tell the foot how big to grow. Having the right perspective propels you to act from your vision and not from other's circumstances.

Man is that foolish creature who tries to get even with his enemies and ahead of his friends. Love looks through a telescope; envy, through a microscope. We underrate or exaggerate that which we do not possess. Don't envy anybody. Every person possesses something no other person has. Develop that one thing and make it outstanding.

God enters by a private door into every individual. He leads each of us by a separate path. No one can build his destiny upon the success of another person. What the small man seeks is in others; what the superior man seeks is in God.

THE ONLY WAY TO SEE IS TO KEEP YOUR EYES ON GOD.

NUGGET #23

The Sky's Not The Limit.

No one can put a limit on you without your permission.

"Eli Whitney was laughed at when he showed his cotton gin. Edison had to install his electric light free of charge in an office building before anyone would even look at it. The first sewing machine was smashed to pieces by a Boston mob. People scoffed at the idea of railroads. People thought that traveling thirty miles an hour would stop the circulation of the blood. Morse had to plead before ten Congresses before they would even look at his telegraph," (Anonymous). Yet for all these men the sky was not the limit.

Beware of those who stand aloof and greet each venture with reproof; the world would stop if things were run by men who say "It can't be done."

"Seek, and ye shall find" (Matt. 7:7). We attain only in proportion to what we attempt. More people are persuaded into believing in nothing than believing too much. Jesus said, "According to your faith be it unto you" (Matt. 9:29). You are never as far from the answer as it first appears. It's never safe or accurate to look into the future without faith.

Tell me what you believe about Jesus, and I will tell you some important facts about your future. What picture of Jesus do you have? Is He merely a good man with good ideas? Or is He the Son of God, our advocate before God, the King of Kings and Lord of Lords?

A lot of people no longer hope for the best, they just hope to avoid the worst. Many of us have heard opportunity knocking at our door, but by the time we unhooked the chain, pushed back the bolt, turned two locks and shut off the burglar alarm—it was gone! Too many people spend their lives looking around, looking down or looking behind, when God says to look up. The sky's not the limit!

TAKE THE LID OFF.

NUGGET #24

Face The Music, And Someday You Will Lead The Band.

Not all obstacles are bad. In fact, an opportunity's favorite disguise is an obstacle. Conflict is simply meeting an obstacle on the road to your answer. The fight is good; it is proof that you haven't quit. The apostle Paul said it best when he wrote, "We are pressed on every side by troubles, but not crushed, and broken. We are perplexed because we don't know why things happen as they do, but we don't give up and quit. We are hunted down, but God never abandons us. We get knocked down, but we get up again and keep going" (2 Cor 4: 8-9, LB).

Being a Christian does not remove you from the world and its problems; rather it equips you to live in it productively and victoriously. No one is immune to problems. Even the lion has to fight off flies. Growth and success don't eliminate obstacles; they create new ones. But God is always working on us and walking with us. Thomas Carlisle said, "The block of granite which was an obstacle in the pathway of the weak becomes a stepping-stone in the pathway of the strong."

Even in the midst of trials, God wants growth and promotion for you. Trials provide an opportunity to grow, not die. Obstacles can temporarily detour you, but only you can make you stop. The devil wants you to think there's nothing more permanent than your temporary situation. Obstacles reveal what we truly believe and who we really are. They introduce you to yourself. Your struggle may be lasting, but it is not everlasting.

As I've traveled, I've always noticed that no matter how cloudy it is when the plane takes off, above the clouds the sun always shines. Look up! It's not your outlook but your "uplook" that counts. Obstacles are a part of life. Jesus said, "In the world ye shall have tribulation: but be of good cheer; I have overcome the world" (John 16:33). Jesus does not say, "There is no storm." He says, "I am here; do not tremble, just trust." The difference between iron and steel is fire, but the fire-tried steel is worth it. God never promised that it would be easy. He did say (Mark 9:24), "all things are possible to him that believeth."

"In the presence of trouble, some people grow wings; others buy crutches," said Harold W. Ruoff. When God is at your side, He helps you face the music, even when you don't like the tune. Don't just look to God through your circumstances; look at your circumstances through God.

YOUR PROBLEM IS
YOUR PROMOTION.

NUGGET #25

You Were Created To Be An Answer.

The great basketball coach John Wooden said, "You cannot live a perfect day without doing something for someone who will never be able to repay you." I believe a powerful scripture in the Bible that releases the blessing of God in your life is Proverbs 3:27, which says, "Withhold not good from them to whom it is due, when it is in the power of thine hand to do it."

Joy shared is joy doubled. You were created to be a part of the solution. "I am only one, but still I am one. I cannot do everything, but still I can do something; I will not refuse to do the something I can do," said Helen Keller.

Be an answer. Get in the way if someone you know is on the way down. Walk in on someone you can help when others are walking out. There are no unimportant jobs, no unimportant people, no unimportant acts of kindness. If you haven't got any kindness in your heart, you have the worst kind of heart trouble.

Your contribution is determined by the answers you give to the problems you face. According to Mike Murdock, "You will only be remembered for two things: the problems you solve or the ones you create." It's always more blessed to give than to receive (Acts 20:35).

Give of yourself to others, and watch criticism leave your life. Critics are usually the most inactive of people. Walk in your neighbor's shoes, sit in your boss's chair, run the path of your best friend. Be on the lookout for ways to be an answer.

How many happy selfish people do you know? You can make more friends in two months by helping other people than you can in two years by trying to get others to help you. "The Dead Sea is a dead sea because it continually receives and never gives." (Anonymous). "If God can get it through you, God will give it to you," says Pastor E.V. Hill. Just one act of yours may be all it takes to turn the tide of another person's life.

FIND THE PROBLEMS
THAT YOU'RE AN
ANSWER TO.

NUGGET #26

Words Are Like Nitroglycerine: They Can Blow Up Bridges Or Heal Hearts.

Just to see how it feels, for the next twenty-four hours refrain from saying anything bad about anyone or anything. "The difference between the right word and the almost right word is the difference between lightning and the lightning bug," said Mark Twain. Proverbs 16:27 (LB) says, "Idle hands are the devil's workshop; idle lips are his mouthpiece." "It is true that life and death are in the power of the tongue" (Prov 18:21).

You can tell more about a person by what he says about others than by what others say about him. Jesus said, "Out of the abundance of the heart the mouth speaketh" (Matt. 12:34). An original person says, "Let's find a way"; a copy says, "There is no way." An original says, "There should be a better way to do it"; a copy says, "That's the way it's always been done." Instead of using the words "if only," try substituting "next time." Don't ask, "What if it doesn't work?" Ask instead, "What if it does?"

Ignorance is always eager to speak. The best time to hold your tongue is when you feel you must say something. You'll never be hurt by anything you didn't say. Silence is the ultimate weapon of power; it is also one of the hardest arguments to dispute. Never judge a person's horsepower by his exhaust. Some people speak from experience; others, from experience, don't speak.

Take a tip from nature – your ears aren't made to shut, but your mouth is! When an argument flares up, the wise man quenches it with silence. Sometimes you have to be quiet to be heard. It's when the fish opens his mouth that he gets caught.

Your words are a reflection of your destiny. Jesus said, "Your words now reflect your fate then: either you will be justified by them or you will be condemned" (Matt. 12:37, LB). The book of Exodus says, "Now go ahead and do as I [the Lord] tell you, for I will help you to speak well, and I will tell you what to say" (Ex. 4:12).

To know a man, listen carefully when he mentions his dislikes. Flapping gums dull your two most important senses–your sight and your hearing. Many a great idea has been quenched by wrong words.

A wise old owl sat on an oak,
The more he saw the less he spoke;
The less he spoke the more he heard;
Why aren't we like that wise old bird?

–Edward H. Richards

EVERY TIME YOU SAY "GOD" YOU SAY "MIRACLE".

NUGGET #27

Unforgiveness Has No Foresight.

Unforgiveness is the one guaranteed formula for smothering our originality. When you have been wronged, a poor memory is your best response. Never carry a grudge. While you're straining under its weight, the other guy's out producing.

Forgive your enemies—nothing annoys them more. There is no revenge so sweet as forgiveness. The only people you should try to get even with are those who have helped you.

"Forgiveness ought to be like a canceled note—torn in two, and burned up, so that it never can be shown against one," (Henry Ward Beecher). Never is God operating in your life so strong as when you forego revenge and dare to forgive an injury. "He who cannot forgive, destroys the bridge over which he may one day need to pass," said Larry Bielat. "Never cut what can be untied," (Joseph Joubert). Hate, bitterness and revenge are luxuries none of us can afford.

People need loving most when they deserve it least. Forgiveness heals; unforgiveness wounds. Matthew 5:25 (LB) says, "Come to terms quickly with your enemy before it is too late." The best healing is a quick healing.

You can't get ahead when you're trying to get even. Being offended is a strategy of Satan's to get you out of the will of God. When we think about our offense, trouble grows; when we think about God, trouble goes.

When you don't forgive, you are ignoring its impact on your destiny. Hate is a prolonged form of suicide of your dreams. How much more grievous are the consequences of unforgiveness than the causes of it!

It's true that the one who forgives ends the quarrel. Patting a fellow on the back is the best way to get a chip off his shoulder. Forgive your enemies–you can't get back at them any other way! Forgiveness saves the expense of anger, the high cost of hatred and the waste of energy. There are two marks of a Christian: giving and forgiving.

If you want to be miserable, hate somebody. Unforgiveness does a great deal more damage to the vessel in which it is stored than the object on which it is poured.

"Life is an adventure in forgiveness," says author Norman Cousins. "Every person should have a special cemetery lot in which to bury the faults of friends and loved ones. To forgive is to set a prisoner free and discover the prisoner was you" (Unknown).

FORGIVE SOMEONE EVERY DAY.

NUGGET #28

What Good Is Aim If You Don't Know When To Pull The Trigger?

God is a God of timing and direction. He wants us to know what to do and when to do it. Psalm 32:8 says, "I will instruct thee and teach thee in the way which thou shalt go: I will guide thee with mine eye." Don't live your life ahead of God's will or outside of His will.

Patience will do wonders, but it was not much help to the man who planted an orange grove in Alaska. There is never a right time to do the wrong thing. If you take too long in deciding what to do with your life, you'll find you've lived it. Time was invented by almighty God in order to give dreams a chance. "Hell is truth seen too late–duty neglected in its season," says Tyron Edwards. Ideas won't keep. Something must be done about them. "There is one thing stronger than all the armies in the world, and that is an idea whose time has come," says Victor Hugo.

Always apply light and not heat to your dreams. God says His "Word is a lamp unto my feet and a light unto my path" (Ps. 119:105). The lamp illuminates things we are dealing with now. The light directs our future.

Jumping to a wrong decision seldom leads to a happy landing. Too many people leave the right opportunity to look for other opportunities. Seize today's opportunities today and tomorrow's opportunities tomorrow.

Don't hurry when success depends on accuracy. Those who make the worst use of their time are the first to complain of its shortness. The fastest running back is useless unless heading toward the right goal line.

Timing is the vital ingredient for success. "For the vision is yet for an appointed time" (Hab. 2:3). There is an appointed time for your vision. Have 20/20 vision; don't be too far-sighted or too near-sighted. As I've studied Godly leaders I have found that at key times they have said, "God led me to do..."

Following His will releases the originality within you and helps you identify priorities. If Jesus is the Way, why waste time traveling some other way?

ASK GOD FOR HIS TIMING AND DIRECTION.

NUGGET #29

Today I Will...

Rise early because no day is long enough for a day's work.

Compliment three people.

Make myself valuable to somebody.

Not lose an hour in the morning and spend all day looking for it.

Tackle a problem bigger than me.

Make a small improvement in some area.

Change my thinking from TGIF to TGIT—Thank God It's Today!

Do at least three things that will take me out of my comfort zone.

Die to myself.

Give thanks for my daily bread.

Find something different to do.

Leave someone a little better than I found them.
Give my best time to communion with God.

Live by the Golden Rule so I won't have to apologize for my actions tomorrow.

Know that the place to be happy is here, the time to be happy is now.

Take small steps to conquer a bad habit.

Judge this day, not by the harvest, but by the seeds I plant.

NUGGET #30

You Were Created For Connection.

God did not write solo parts for us. He has divine connections for you—the right friends and the right associations.
These good connections always bring out the original in you. You
know the kind of people I'm talking about. After you've been with
them you find yourself less critical, more full of faith and with a
vision for the future.

It is very important who we closely associate with. Have you ever
known a backslider who didn't first hang around the wrong kind
of people? The devil doesn't use strangers to deter or stop you.
These wrong associations bring out the worst in you, not the best.
After you're around them you'll find yourself full of doubt, fear,
confusion and criticism.

As you grow in God your associations will change. Some of your
friends will not want you to go on. They will want you to stay
where they are. Friends who don't help you climb, will want you to
crawl. Your friends will stretch your vision or choke your dream.

Never let anyone talk you out of pursuing a God-given idea.
"Don't let someone else create your world for you, for when they
do, they always make it too small," says men's minister Edwin
Louis Cole. Who's creating your world? Never receive counsel from
unproductive people. Never discuss your problems with someone
incapable of contributing to the solution.

Those who never succeed themselves are always first to tell you how. Not everyone has a right to speak into your life. You are certain to get the worst of the bargain when you exchange ideas with the wrong person. Don't follow anyone who's not going anywhere. We are to follow no person further than he or she follows Jesus.

"When God gets ready to bless you, He brings a person into your life," says Mike Murdock. Respect those whom God has connected to you to help you. God cares for people through people.

With some people you spend an evening; with others you invest it. Be careful where you stop to inquire for directions along the road of life. Wise is the man who fortifies his life with the right friendships.

YOU DO BECOME LIKE THOSE YOU CLOSELY ASSOCIATE WITH.

NUGGET #31

Turn Into Stepping Stones The Bricks Others Throw At You.

All great ideas create conflict. In other words, your destiny creates challenges and criticism. Every great idea has three stages of responses:

- "It is impossible—don't waste the time and the money."
- "It is possible but has a limited value."
- "I said it was a good idea all along."

Our response to critics should be what the Bible says in 2 Corinthians 4:8-9: "We are perplexed, but not in despair; persecuted, but not forsaken; cast down, but not destroyed."

Criticism of Christians is the language of the devil. The Bible says the devil is the accuser of the brethren. Therefore, we should consider that "He that is without sin among you, let him cast the first stone" (John 8:7). Attention men: Before you criticize another, look closely at your sister's brother!

It is the still small voice that we should follow, not the screeching blasts of doom. Criticism is always a part of supernatural promotion. If your head sticks up above the crowd, expect more criticism than bouquets Satan always attacks those who can hurt him the most. God works from the inside out; the devil tries to work from the outside in.

Whoever criticizes to you will criticize about you. If someone belittles you, he is only trying to cut you down to his size. A statue has never been set up to a critic.

You can always tell a failure by the way he criticizes success. Those who can—do. Those who can't—criticize. Those who complain about the way the ball bounces are often the ones who dropped it. If it were not for the doers, the critics would soon be out of business. Envy provides the mud that failures throw at success. Critics that throw mud are simultaneously losing ground. Small minds are the first to condemn great ideas.

If people talk negatively about you, live so that no one will believe them. Fear of criticism is the kiss of death in the courtship of achievement. If you are afraid of criticism, you'll die doing nothing. A successful man is one who can lay a firm foundation with the bricks that others throw at him.

CRITICISM IS A COMPLIMENT WHEN YOU'RE FOLLOWING GOD'S PLAN.

NUGGET #32

There Is No Such Thing As A Self-Made Man.

No one makes it alone. Remember, if you try to go it alone, then the fence that shuts others out shuts you in. "God sends no one away except those who are full of themselves," (D.L. Moody). The man who only works by himself and for himself is likely to be corrupted by the company he keeps.

"Everyone who has ever done a kind deed for us, or spoken one word of encouragement to us, has entered into the make-up of our character and of our thoughts, as well as our success," says George Matthew Adams. Have a grateful heart and be quick to acknowledge those who help you. Make yourself indispensable to somebody. It is easy to blame others for your failures, but do you credit others with your successes?

"Tunnel vision tells you nobody is working as hard as you are. It is an enemy of teamwork. It is a door through which division and strife enter," (Tim Redmond). Few burdens are heavy when everybody lifts. Freckles would make a nice tan if they would get together.

The man who believes in nothing but himself lives in a very small world—one in which few will want to enter. The man who sings his own praises may have the right tune but the wrong lyrics. The higher you go in life, the more dependent you become on other people. A conceited person never gets anywhere because he thinks he is already there.

Work together with others. Remember the banana: Every time it leaves the bunch, it gets peeled and eaten. You'll never experience lasting success without relationships with people. No one person alone can match the cooperative effort of the right team. "We" makes "me" stronger.

FIND SOMEONE WHO CAN HELP YOU.

NUGGET #33

A Smile Is Mightier Than A Grin.

The most bankrupt person in the world is the one who has lost his joy. Decide to become the most positive and enthusiastic person you know.

In a recent survey two hundred national leaders were asked what makes a person successful. Eighty percent listed enthusiasm as the most important quality. A person who is enthusiastic soon has enthusiastic followers.

How many people do you know who became successful doing something they hate? "Find something you love to do, and you'll never have to work another day in your life," says author Harvey Mackay. Thomas Carlisle said, "Give me a man who sings at his work." That's the kind of people I want to hire!

"Keep your face to the sunshine and you cannot see the shadow," said Helen Keller. The unwise person seeks happiness in the future; the wise person grows it today. There is no sadder sight than a Christian pessimist. Your world will look brighter from behind a smile. A smile is the shortest distance between two people.

Happiness is always an inside job. Our first choice is to rejoice. "And we know that all that happens to us is working for our good if we love God and are fitting into his plans" (Rom. 8:28, LB). "Happy is that people whose God is the Lord" (Ps. 144:15). God's joy is contagious.

Greet the unseen with a cheer, not a fear. "Laughter is a form of internal jogging. It moves your internal organs around. It enhances respiration. It is an igniter of great expectations," says Norman Cousins. God says in His Word, "If you don't praise me, the rocks will." Let's not be replaced by a bunch of rocks!

For every minute you're angry, you lose sixty seconds of happiness. Two things contribute to happiness: What we can do without, and what we can do with. People are about as happy as they make up their minds to be. Happiness can never be found, because it was never lost. Be like the steam kettle! Though up to its neck in hot water, it continues to sing.

SMILE, IT ADDS TO YOUR FACE VALUE.

LOOKING
UPWARD

NUGGET #34

If You Pluck The Blossoms, You Must Do Without the Fruit.

God is a God of seasons. "To everything there is a season, and a time to every purpose under the heaven" says Ecclesiastes 3:1. Distinctly different things happen during different seasons.

There is a wintertime in God. It is a season of preparation, revelation and direction. It is also the time when the roots grow. God wants to establish the right foundation in you during this season. But there is no harvest now.

There is a springtime in God. It is a time of planting, hoeing and nurturing. In other words, hard work. God wants you to work your plan. But there is no harvest in springtime.

There is a summertime in God. Summer is a time of great growth. Now is the time when activity, interest and people begin to surround your God-given idea. For all the activity of summer, there is only a minimal harvest. But then comes autumn.

This is God's harvest time. It is during this season that the harvest is reaped in much greater proportion than the work or activity expended. But most people never make it to the fall. Often they end up quitting along the way because they don't know what season they're in.

When you understand that God is a God of seasons, it prepares you to do the right thing at the right time. It inspires you to persevere to the fall. God's Word is true when it says, "Let us not become weary in doing good, for at the proper time we will reap a harvest if we do not give up" (Gal 6:9, NIV).

It was spring, but it was summer I wanted,
the warm days, and the great outdoors.
It was summer, but it was fall I wanted,
the colorful leaves, and the cool, dry air.
It was spring, but it was winter I wanted,
the beautiful snow, and the joy of the holiday season.
I was a child, but it was adulthood I wanted,
the freedom, and the respect.
I was twenty, but it was thirty I wanted,
to be mature, and sophisticated.
I was middle-aged, but it was thirty I wanted,
the youth, and the free spirit.
I was retired, but it was middle age I wanted,
the presence of mind, without limitations.
My life was over,
but I never got what I wanted.

–Jason Lehman

God has the right time and season for you.

STAY IN SEASON WITH GOD.

NUGGET #35

One Action Is More Valuable Than A Thousand Good Intentions.

"As He [Jesus] was speaking, a woman in the crowd called out, 'God bless your mother—the womb from which you came, and the breasts that gave you suck!' He replied, 'Yes, but even more blessed are all who hear the Word of God and put it into practice" (Luke 11:27, LB). It is more blessed to be a doer of the Word of God than even to have been the mother of Jesus.

Few dreams come true by themselves. The test of a person lies in action. No one ever stumbled onto something big while sitting down. Even a fly doesn't get a slap on the back until he starts to work. A famous anonymous poem says, "Sitting still and wishing makes no person great; the good Lord sends the fishing, but you must dig the bait."

Realize that nothing is learned while you talk. Words without actions are the assassins of dreams. The smallest good deed is better than the greatest intention. History is made whenever you take the right action. Action is the proper fruit of knowledge. Getting an idea should be like sitting on a tack—it should make you jump up and do something.

"Go to the ant, thou sluggard; consider her ways, and be wise: which having no guide, overseer, or ruler, provideth her meat in the summer, and gathereth her food in the harvest" (Prov. 6:6-8).

"Nothing preaches better than this ant, yet she says nothing," (Ben Franklin). You earn respect only by action; inaction earns disrespect.

Some people find life an empty dream because they put nothing into it. Every time one person expresses an idea, he finds ten others who thought of it before—but took no action. Mark Twain said, "Thunder is good, thunder is impressive, but it is lightning that does the work." The test of this book is that the reader goes away saying, not "What a lovely book" but, "I will do something!"

The devil is willing for you to confess faith as long as you don't practice it. When praying, we must simultaneously be willing to take the action that God directs in the answer to our prayer. The answers to your prayers will include action.

The Bible tells us that action gives life to faith (see James 2:26). Even a child is known by his doings (Prov. 20:11). Many churchgoers sing "Standing on the Promises" when all they are doing is sitting on the premises. Too many people avoid discovering the secret of success because deep down they suspect the secret may be hard work.

ACT NOW ON GOD'S DIRECTION.

NUGGET #36

Adopt The Pace Of God.

God is a planner, a strategist. He is incredibly organized and has a definite pace. More like a marathon runner than a sprinter, He has our whole lives in mind, not just tomorrow. Remember God is never late. Never try to hurry God. "He that believeth shall not make haste," the Bible says in Isaiah 28:16. Urgent matters are seldom urgent. Pressure usually accompanies us when we are out of the pace of God.

Proverbs 16:9 (LB) says, "We should make plans, counting on God to direct us." Proverbs 16:3 (NIV) tells us, "Commit to the Lord whatever you do, and your plans will succeed." Cowards never start, and the lukewarm die along the way. God is the original's hope and the copy's excuse. Is God your hope or your excuse?

Adopt the pace of God; His secret is patience. There is no time lost in waiting if you are waiting on the Lord. The road to success runs uphill, so don't expect to break any speed records. All great achievements require time. Happiness is a direction, not a destination.

Abraham Lincoln, during the darkest hours of the Civil War, said in response to the question whether he was sure God was on his side, "I do not know: I have not thought about that. But I am very anxious to know whether we are on God's side." "The strength of a man consists in finding out the way God is going, and going that way," said Henry Ward Beecher.

Walking in the pace of God helps establish us on the proper foundation. Nothing is permanent unless it is built on God's will and God's Word. "Except the Lord build the house, they labor in vain that build it" (Ps. 127:1). "The steps of a good man are ordered by the Lord, and he delighteth in his way," (Ps. 37:23). Never remain where God has not sent you.

A Christian with the right pace is like a candle, which must keep cool and burn at the same time. (But if you burn the candle at both ends, you are not as bright as you think).

Every great person first learned how to obey, whom to obey and when to obey. A famous anonymous poem says, "The place I choose, or place I shun, my soul is satisfied with none; but when Thy will directs my way, 'tis equal joy to go or stay."

GOD HAS YOUR WHOLE LIFE IN MIND WHEN HE DIRECTS YOU.

NUGGET #37

The Alphabet For Originality.

A

attitude

B

believer

C

character

D

decisive

E

effort

F

fearless

G

gratitude

H

honesty

I

ideas

J

joy

K

kind-hearted

L

leadership

M

merciful

N

nonconformity

O

objectives

P

pray

Q

quiet-time

R

responsibility

S

sensitivity

T

tenacity

U

unhesitating

V

vigilant

W

wholehearted

X

e(x)ceptional

Y

yielded

Z

zealous

NUGGET #38

In The Race For Excellence There Is No Finish Line.

Commit yourself to excellence from the start. No legacy is so rich as excellence. The quality of your life will be in direct proportion to your commitment to excellence, regardless of what you choose to do. "It's a funny thing about life; if you refuse to accept anything but the best, you very often get it," said Somerset Maugham. It takes less time to do something right than it does to explain why you did it wrong. "There is an infinite difference between a little wrong and just right, between fairly good and the best, between mediocrity and superiority," said Orison Swett Marcen.

Every day we should ask ourselves, "Why should my boss hire me instead of someone else?" or "Why should people do business with me instead of my competitors?" "Watch your actions; they become habits. Watch your habits; they become character. Watch your character; it becomes your destiny," said Frank Outlaw.

"Sin has many tools, but a lie is the handle that fits them all," said Oliver Wendell Holmes. Those who are given to white lies soon become color blind. A lie has no legs to support itself—it requires other lies. When you stretch the truth, watch out for the snap back. Each time you lie, even a little white lie, you push yourself toward failure. However, each time you are honest, you propel yourself toward greater success.

Outside forces don't control your character. You do. The measure of a person's real character is what he would do if he knew he would never be found out. Be more concerned with your character than with your reputation because your character is what you really are while your reputation is merely what others think you are. There is no right way to do the wrong thing.

"He that is good will infallibly become better, and he that is bad will as certainly become worse; for vice, virtue and time are three things that never stand still," said Charles Caleb Colton. Recently I saw a plaque that said, "Excellence can be attained if you...Care more than others think is wise, Risk more than others think is safe, Dream more than others think is practical, Expect more than others think is possible." Excellence—it's contagious...be a leader...start an epidemic!

COMMIT YOURSELF TO EXCELLING AT EXCELLENCE.

NUGGET #39

Is God Finished With You Yet?

If you are still breathing, the answer is no. Don't die until you're dead. Psalm 138:8 says, "The Lord will perfect that which concerneth me." God is continually perfecting and fine-tuning each of us. He wants to fulfill all of His promises and purposes in our lives.

Romans 11:29 (NIV) says "for God's gifts and his call are irrevocable." What God has put in you stays your whole life. He still wants to use them in order to fulfill His plan for your life.

"The creation of a thousand forests is in one acorn," said Ralph Waldo Emerson. The creation of your destiny is held within the seeds of your God-given gifts and calling.

God begins with a positive and ends with a positive. "Being confident of this, that he who began a good work in you will carry it on to completion until the day of Christ Jesus" (Phil 1:6, NIV). Jesus hasn't come back, so that means God isn't finished with you. God's will for us is momentum, building from one good work to another.

Don't just go on to other things, go on to higher things. The pains of being a Christian are all growing pains, and those growing pains lead to maturity. God's way becomes plain as we walk in it. When faith is stretched, it grows. "The more we do the more we can do," said William Hazlitt.

Greater opportunity and momentum is the reward of past accomplishment. Success makes failures out of too many people when they stop after a victory. When we do what we can, God will do what we can't. He's not finished with you!

WHAT YOU THOUGHT WAS DEAD STILL HAS LIFE.

NUGGET #40

Believe Six Impossible Things Before Breakfast.

Imagine beginning tomorrow as you have never done before. Instead of just stretching your body when you get out of bed, stretch your very being with all of the good things God has in store for you. Think, plan, believe and pray for things that require God's involvement.

Grab hold of each day from the start. Most people lose an hour at the beginning of the day and spend the rest of the day trying to recapture it. The first hour of the morning is the rudder of the day. Never begin your day in neutral. Take the offensive. Create a habit of initiative. It's the person who doesn't need a boss that's usually selected to be one. When you're a self- starter, others don't have to be a crank.

Duties delayed are the devil's delight. The devil doesn't care what your plans are as long as you don't do anything about them. You will never gain what you are unwilling to go after. The key to your future is hidden in your daily approach to life.

Seize your destiny. Don't let it slip away. "If God has called you, don't look over your shoulder to see who is following you," (Anonymous). "Let every man abide in the same calling wherein he was called" (1 Cor. 7:20). "The crude and physical agony of the cross was nothing compared to the indifference of the crowd on

Main Street as Jesus passed by," said Allan Knight Chalmers. Don't live an indifferent life as if Jesus did nothing for you.

Satan trembles when he sees the weakest Christian taking the offensive. "The breakfast of Christian champions is early morning prayer," says Billy Joe Daugherty. God is worth your time. Bring God on the scene from the start and you'll always finish strong.

START YOUR DAY RIGHT
AND NEVER LOOK BACK.

NUGGET #41

You'll Always Be More Convinced By What You've Discovered Than By What Others Have Found.

Go from being dependent on others to being dependent on God. He is the source of our direction. Yet too many people base what they believe, do and say on what others believe, do and say. Revelation is only revelation when it's your revelation. God is best known by revelation, not explanation.

Obviously, God uses ministers, Christian leaders, books, Christian TV, tapes and other ways to speak truth into our lives. But it is not enough that what they say is right. Faith will only work when we believe it for ourselves and place a demand on it. If another person's faith can't gain your entrance to heaven, it can't gain your destiny either.

There are two kinds of unwise people: One says, "This is old, therefore it is good." The other says, "This is new, therefore it is better." Do not attempt something unless you are sure of it yourself; but do not abandon it because someone else is not sure of you.

The most important convictions in our lives cannot be reached on the word of another. "The Bible is so simple you have to have someone else help you misunderstand it," says Charles Capps. Theologians are always trying to make the Bible a book without common sense. God did make it easy to find out for ourselves.

John Wesley said it best when he said, "When I was young, I was sure of everything; in a few years, having been mistaken a thousand times, I was not half so sure of most things as I was before; at present, I am hardly sure of anything but what God has revealed to me."

GO FROM KNOWING WHAT OTHERS BELIEVE TO KNOWING WHAT YOU BELIEVE.

NUGGET #42

Something Dominates Everyone's Day.

What influence dominates your day? Is it the daily news, your negative neighbor, the memory of a failure? Or is it God's plan for you, His Word in your heart, a song of praise to Him? Let the plan that God has for your life dominate your day, or something else will.

Mediocrity has its own type of intensity. It wants to dominate your day. It can influence and affect every area of your life if you let it. "Some temptations come to the industrious, but all temptations attack the idle," (Charles Spurgeon).

A fruitful life is not the result of chance. It is the result of right choices. Small mounds of dirt add up to a mountain. If you are not alert to pray, the mountain can dominate your day.

When the news tries to dominate your day, let the good news dominate your day.

When the past tries to dominate your day, let your dreams dominate your day.

When fear tries to dominate your day, let right action dominate your day.

When procrastination tries to dominate your day, let small steps dominate your day.

When wrong influences try to dominate your day, let the right associations dominate your day.

When confusion tries to dominate your day, let God's Word dominate your day.

When loneliness tries to dominate your day, let prayer dominate your day.

When strife tries to dominate your day, let peace dominate your day.

When your mind tries to dominate your day, let The Spirit dominate your day.

When envy tries to dominate your day, let blessing others dominate your day.

When greed tries to dominate your day, let giving dominate your day.

LET GOD DOMINATE YOUR DAY.

NUGGET #43

Once You've Found A Better Way, Make That Way Better.

All progress is due to those who were not satisfied to let well enough alone. "Acorns were good until bread was found," said Sir Francis Bacon. The majority of men meet with failure because of their lack of persistence in creating new plans to improve those that succeed.

If at first you do succeed, try something harder. There is no mistake so great as the mistake of quitting after a victory. If you can't think up a new idea, find a way to make better use of an old one. "Where we cannot invent, we may at least improve," said Charles Caleb Colton.

Don't look for the answer to your problem; look for many answers, then choose the best one. The guy who moves ahead is the one who does more than is required and continues doing it. "The difference between ordinary and extraordinary is that little extra," says Zig Ziglar.

There is always a way—there is always a better way. When you've found something—look again. School is never out! The more you truly desire something, the more you will try to find a better way.

The deeper we go in God, the deeper He goes in us. "A wise man will hear, and will increase learning" (Prov. 1:5). The biggest enemy of best is good. If you're satisfied with what's good, you'll never have what's best.

"It's what you learn after you know it all that counts," says John Wooden. The man who thinks he knows it all has merely stopped thinking. If you think you've arrived, you'll be left behind. A successful man continues to look for work after he has found a job.

Cause something to happen. "Show me a thoroughly satisfied man, and I will show you a failure," said Thomas Edison. "There are two kinds of men who never amount to very much," Cyrus H.K. Curtis remarked to his associate, Edward Bok. "And what kinds are those?" inquired Bok. "Those who cannot do what they are told," replied the famous publisher, "and those who can do nothing else." Find a better way, and make that way better.

GOD ALWAYS HAS A BETTER WAY.

NUGGET #44

God Made You...

God made you different, not indifferent.

God made you extraordinary, not ordinary.

God made you significant, not insignificant.

God made you competent, not incompetent.

God made you compatible, not incompatible.

God made you active, not inactive.

God made you indispensable, not dispensable.

God made you effective, not defective.

God made you adept, not inept.

God made you distinct, not indistinct.

God made you adequate, not inadequate.

God made you efficient, not inefficient.

God made you superior, not inferior

God made you responsible, not irresponsible

God made you solvent, not insolvent

God made you sane, not insane

God made you efficient, not deficient

God made you consistent, not inconsistent

God made you insightful, not despiteful

God made you irresistible, not resistible

God made you sensitive, not insensitive

God made you uncommon, not common

God made you decisive, not indecisive

God made you an original, not a copy

NUGGET #45

The Worst Buy
Is An Alibi.

Excuses are the nails used to build a house of failure. An alibi is worse and more terrible than a lie, for an alibi is a lie guarded. Ninety-nine percent of failures come from people who have the habit of making excuses.

When you're good at making excuses, it's hard to excel at anything else. Don't make excuses, make progress. Excuses always replace progress. A person may fail many times, but he isn't a failure until he blames somebody or something else.

There may be many reasons for failure, but not a single excuse. Never let a challenge become an alibi. You have a choice: You can let the obstacle be an alibi or an opportunity. No alibi will ever serve the purpose of God.

An alibi is egotism wrong-side-out. Those who are unfaithful will always find an alibi. The person who really wants to do something finds a way; the other finds an excuse.

Excuses always precipitate failure. "Bread of deceit is sweet to a man; but afterwards his mouth shall be filled with gravel" (Prov. 20:17).

It's been said that an excuse is a thin skin of falsehood stretched tightly over a bald-faced lie. For every sin Satan is ready to provide an excuse.

Success is a matter of luck. Ask any failure. There are always enough excuses available if you are weak enough to use them. Don't buy that alibi.

EXCHANGE YOUR ALIBIS
FOR OPPORTUNITIES.

NUGGET #46

The Doors Of Opportunity Are Marked "Push."

Get aggressive and go after opportunities. They may not find you. The reason some people don't go very far in life is because they sidestep opportunity and shake hands with procrastination. Procrastination is the grave in which opportunity is buried. Don't be caught out in the backyard looking for four-leaf clovers when opportunity knocks at your front door. For the tenacious there is always time and opportunity.

Watch for big problems; they disguise big opportunities. Opposition, distraction and challenges always surround the birth of a dream. Make the most of all that comes and the least of all that goes. Adversity is fertile soil for creativity.

To the alert Christian, interruptions are only divinely inserted opportunities. Life's disappointments are opportunity's hidden appointments. When God prepares to do something wonderful, He begins with a difficulty. When He plans to do something very wonderful, He begins with an impossibility!

"A wise man will make more opportunities than he finds," said Francis Bacon. It's more valuable to find a situation that redistributes opportunity than one that redistributes wealth. Have you ever noticed that great people are never lacking for opportunities? When successful people are interviewed, they always mention their big plans for the future. Most of us would think., "If I were in their shoes, I'd kick back and do nothing." Success doesn't diminish their dreams.

There is far more opportunity than ability. Life is full of golden opportunities for doing what we are called to do. Every person has a lot that he can do. Start with what you can do; don't stop because of what you can't do.

Greater opportunities and joy come to those who make the most of small ones. In the parable of the talents the master told the servant who used what he had, "Well done, good and faithful servant; thou hast been faithful over a few things, I will make thee ruler over many things: enter thou into the joy of thy lord" (Matt 25:23).

Many people seem to think that opportunity means a chance to get money without earning it. God's best gifts to us are not things, but opportunities. And those doors of opportunity are marked "push."

BREAK THROUGH THOSE ARTIFICIAL BARRIERS TO NEW OPPORTUNITIES.

NUGGET #47

Expand Your Horizons.

We all live under the same sky, but we don't all have the same horizon. Originals always see a bigger picture. Expanding your horizons means being able to see the greater potential that's all around you. When you expand your horizons your life view will change. You will begin to see things around you differently.

The world's demands don't control the Christian's supply. "Don't be afraid to take a big step if one is indicated. You can't cross a chasm in two small jumps," (Unknown). "Aim at the sun and you may not reach it, but your arrow will fly far higher than if aimed at an object on a level with yourself," says Joel Hawes.

A woman's horizons were changed forever when she came up to Picasso in a restaurant and asked him to scribble something on her napkin. She said she'd be happy to pay him whatever he felt it was worth. Picasso did what she asked and then said, "That will be $10,000." "But you did that in only thirty seconds," the woman exclaimed. "No," Picasso said, "it has taken me forty years to do that."

"If the son [of God] therefore shall make you free, ye shall be free indeed" (John 8:36). Knowing Jesus brings freedom, and freedom releases you to think and see higher. Vision is the art of seeing things that are unseen.

If what you did yesterday still looks big to you, you haven't done much today (The Sunday School). You will never learn faith in easy circumstances. When God stretches you, you never snap back to your original shape. He who is afraid of doing too much always does too little. Make sure the road you're on is not leading to a cul-desac.

"Man cannot discover new oceans unless he has courage to lose sight of the shore," (Anonymous). That's why Jesus said, "Launch out into the deep!" (Luke 5:4). Enough spiritual power is going to waste to put Niagara Falls to shame. Unless you try to see beyond what you have already seen, you will never grow.

LOOK AROUND...THEN LOOK A LITTLE FARTHER...THEN LOOK A LITTLE FARTHER STILL.

NUGGET #48

Good Intentions Aren't Good Enough.

You can't test your destiny cautiously. "Don't play for safety — it's the most dangerous thing in the world," said Hugh Walpole. The key is this: to forfeit the safety of what we are for what we could become. Unless you do something beyond what you have already done, you will never grow.

A definition of "mediocrity": best of the worst and worst of the best. "Potential" means you haven't done your best yet. Good intentions are like checks that men try to draw from a bank where they have no account. Every mediocre person has good intentions.

It's been said that the biggest enemy of great is good. Don't accept good enough as good enough. Tolerating mediocrity in others makes me more mediocre. Only an average person is always at his best.

A man can't make a place for himself in the sun if he keeps taking refuge under the family tree. Go! Launch out! "People who never do any more than they get paid for never get paid for any more than they do," said Elbert Hubbard. Do more!

An over-cautious person burns bridges of opportunity before he gets to them. Most of the people who sit around and wait for the harvest haven't planted anything. The average man doesn't want much and usually gets even less.

One action is more valuable than a thousand good intentions. "Security is mostly a superstition. It does not exist in nature, nor do the children of men as a whole experience it. Avoiding danger is no safer in the long run than outright exposure. Life is either a daring adventure, or nothing" (Helen Keller).

GO FROM GOOD INTENTIONS
TO GOOD BEGINNINGS

NUGGET #49

Don't Miss The Silver Lining Only Looking For The Gold.

Jesus never taught men how to make a living. He taught men how to live. "God doesn't call us to be successful. He calls us to be faithful," said Albert Hubbard. Most people have their eye on the wrong goal. Is more money, a higher position or more influence your goal? These are not true goals, but rather simply by-products of goals.

What is a true goal? It is this. "Do not let this Book of the Law depart from your mouth; meditate on it day and night, so that you may be careful to do everything written in it. Then you will be prosperous and successful" (Josh. 1:8, NIV). We should work to become, not to acquire.

Seek not success. Instead, seek the truth, and you will find both. "But seek ye first the kingdom of God, and his righteousness; and all these things shall be added unto you" (Matt. 6:33).

"Happiness is not a reward–it is a consequence. Suffering is not a punishment–it is a result," said Robert Green Ingersoll. Do the very best you can, and leave the results to God. Potential is the most empty word in the world, but with God it can be filled to overflowing.

How small a portion of earth will keep those who are dead, who ambitiously sought after the whole world while they were living! "And how does a man benefit if he gains the whole world and loses his soul in the process?" (Mark 8:36, LB). People are funny; they spend money they don't have, to buy things they don't need, to impress people they don't like.

Success lies not in achieving what you aim at but in aiming at what you ought to achieve. Do what God wants you to do, and He will take care of the rest.

SEEK GOD FIRST AND THE THINGS YOU WANT WILL SEEK YOU.

NUGGET #50

Invest In Yourself.

God, on a regular basis, sends across our paths divine opportunities for investment in ourselves. Be on the lookout for them. He does this first through His Word, which is the best investment we can put into ourselves. But He also sends many other "investment opportunities" to us. In my own life, I've incorporated many of these. For example, my wife and I have a weekly "date night" which has been a great investment in our marriage. Also, every Saturday the kids and I "sneak out" on Mom to an early breakfast together. This time has been great for the kids and me, while allowing my wife a nice break.

Everything you say or do creates an investment somewhere. Whether that investment generates a dividend or a loss depends on you. Always do your best, for what you plant now you will harvest later.

One of the biggest mistakes you can make is to believe that you work for someone else. No matter how many bosses you may have, you really work for the Lord. You can't look to others as your source. That's why tapping into God's investment opportunities is so important. They are one of His ways of developing and instructing us. When an archer misses the mark, he looks for the fault within himself, not within the target. "To improve your aim—improve yourself," (Gilbert Arland).

When prosperity comes, do not use all of it. Give some back to others, and invest some in yourself. One half of knowing what you want is knowing what you must give up before you get it. Time invested in improving yourself precludes time wasted in disapproving others.

"Study to show thyself approved unto God, a workman that needeth not to be ashamed" (2 Tim. 2:15). Investment doesn't cost, it pays. You cannot fulfill your destiny without applying the principle of investing in yourself.

SEIZE THE OPPORTUNITIES GOD SENDS TO INVEST IN YOURSELF.

NUGGET #51

Expect The Opposite.

One of the major reasons the Bible was written was to teach us to expect the opposite of what we see in the world. Indeed, "I can't believe my eyes" is a very spiritual statement, for we are called to walk by faith and not by sight. One of God's principles of opposites is found in John 3:30: "He [Jesus] must increase, but I must decrease." God tells us we must give to receive, die to live and serve to lead. In this world of opposites—what Pat Robertson calls "the upside-down kingdom"—"He who goes to and fro weeping...shall indeed come again with a shout of joy" (Ps. 126:6, NAS), and "He that loseth his life for my [Jesus'] sake shall find it" (Matt 10:39).

When fear comes, expect the opposite – faith to rise up inside you.

When symptoms attack your body, expect the opposite – God's healing power to touch you.

When sadness tries to attach itself to you, expect the opposite – joy to flood your being.

When lack comes in, expect the opposite – God's provision to meet your needs.

When confusion comes, expect the opposite – God's peace to comfort you.

When darkness tries to cover you, expect the opposite – God's light to shine on you.

God chooses ordinary men and women for extraordinary work. "You see your calling , brethren, how that not many wise men after the flesh, not many mighty, not many noble, are called: But God hath chosen the foolish things of the world to confound the wise, and God hath chosen the weak things of the world to confound the things which are mighty...that no flesh should glory in His presence" (1 Cor 1:26-27, 29).

In the midst of your destiny, if you feel unwise and weak, fret not. God is getting ready to move on your behalf and use you. The Sermon on the Mount was preached to lift us out of the Valley of Discouragement. If you want to go higher, go deeper.

This famous poem said it best:

Doubt sees the obstacles
Faith sees the way.
Doubt sees the darkest night
Faith sees the day.
Doubt dreads to take a step
Faith soars on high.
Doubt questions "who believes?"
Faith answers "I."

–Anonymous

LOOKS ARE DECEIVING, ESPECIALLY FIRST IMPRESSIONS OF YOUR PROBLEMS.

NUGGET #52

Memo:

To: You

From: God

Date: Today

Re: What I think about you

I want to tell you that I have known you since before the foundations of time. I even know the hairs on your head. I put you together on purpose and for a purpose. I looked at you and saw that you were fearfully and wonderfully made. I even created you in my image.

I know the plans that I have for you. Plans to prosper and not to harm you. Plans to give you a hope and a future.

I also gave you gifts to prepare and equip you for the plans I have for you. These gifts I've given are irrevocable. Don't neglect them. Exercise them and stir them up!

I want you to be confident about this: When I begin a good work in you I will carry it on to completion until the day of Christ Jesus.

Although you may encounter tribulations in this world, I want you to know that in me you have peace. Be of good cheer. I have overcome the world.

I am not slack concerning my promises. Forever my Word is settled in heaven and my faithfulness to all generations. When I have spoken it, I will also bring it to pass; When I've purposed it, I will also do it.

You can look to me as a refuge and strength, a very present help in trouble. Cast your burdens upon me and I will sustain you. I shall never suffer the righteous to be moved. Come unto me when you labor and are heavy laden, and I will give you rest. For I am your rock, your fortress, your deliverer, your strength in whom you can trust. Though you fall you shall not be utterly cast down, for I will uphold you with my hand.

Don't listen to the ungodly, don't stand with sinners and don't sit with the scornful. But rather delight yourself all day long in my Word. If you do, you will be like a tree planted by the river. You will bring forth fruit in season and whatever you do will prosper.

Finally, I want you to know I love you. I love you so much I gave my only begotten Son. When you believe in Him, you will not die but have healing, freedom, victory, forgiveness, and eternal life.

A FINAL WORD

Be the original person God intended you to be. Don't settle for anything less. Don't look back. Look forward and decide today to take steps toward His plan for your life.

And remember 1 Thessalonians 5:24 that says, "Faithful is he that calleth you, who also will do it."

Additional copies of
You're Born An Original; Don't Die A Copy!
are available at fine bookstores everywhere
or directly from:

Insight International
P.O. Box 54996
Tulsa, Oklahoma 74155

Volume discounts available

John Mason welcomes the opportunity to minister to your church, in conferences, retreats, or in men's, women's, and youth groups.

Available from Insight International are the following:

VIDEOS:

"Momentum: How To Get It, How To Have It, How To Keep It."

"The Good Things About Bad Things."

"Don't Quit."

CASSETTE TAPE SERIES:

"An Enemy Called Average"

"You're Born An Original; Don't Die A Copy!"

BOOKS:

An Enemy Called Average

You're Born An Original; Don't Die A Copy!

About the Author

John Mason is the founder and president of Insight International. His ministry exhorts believers to exercise all of their gifts and talents while fulfilling God's whole plan for their lives. He is the author of several leadership manuals and tape series. He holds a Bachelor of Science degree in Business Administration from Oral Roberts University.

He also has the call and a powerful anointing to preach and minister to churches, men's and women's organizations and other Christian groups.

John was blessed to be raised in a Christian home in Fort Wayne, Indiana, by his parents Chet and Lorene Mason. He, his wife, Linda, and their four children Michelle, Greg, Mike and David currently reside in Orlando, Florida.